Faith 201:
The Great Awakening of Calculated Moves

Atlanta, GA

ISBN: 9781944901295

Copyright © 2025 by Speaking Freedom LLC
All rights reserved.
No portion of this book may be reproduced without written permission from the publisher or author, except as permitted by U.S. copyright law.

Book Cover by: Kaci Winslow

Publisher Website: speakingfreedom.org

Other Website Information:
SpeakingfreedomTV.org, edu-freedom.org

Publisher Address: 75 Washington St. #1177, Fairburn, GA 30213

Speaking Freedom Books' Disclaimers

Welcome to Faith 201: Calculated Moves

We thank you for your purchase and look forward to helping you grow in all areas of your life.

We hope that you find all the information needed for your growth. God bless. Please listen to all disclaimers provided.

If you are currently under a physician's care, please maintain that relationship. This audiobook is not intended to stop your current treatment plan. If you need physician's care, please seek out medical attention.

Please note that all results are based on the individual's ability to adapt and adjust to any given environment or situation. We are not responsible for your results. The life enhancement coaches at Speaking Freedom provide information to help you grow.

You are responsible for maintaining that growth, taking on and applying the information to your individual life as you deem needed and necessary.

This book was written by Speaking Freeodm Books, concept by Kaci (Winslow)Myers.

Please use parental discretion. For best results, you will need an open mind, the ability to research, and a balanced lifestyle.

Section 1: The Introduction

This introduction is intended to help you set your intentions. In this book, we set intentions on your "five year plans." The goal for setting your intentions as you listen to this book is to have in mind the five- year plans that you plan to accomplish and be able to use the tools in this book and the book previously to help you understand how to adjust your faith to reach those goals.

In this particular book, we are going to ask you a different set of questions. If you could be anything you wanted to in the next five years, what would you like to become? What steps would you take to get there? Who would be on your team or what type of team do you think that you need? If you are listening to these questions, hopefully, you've already written down the five-year plan. If not, please use this to help you write your five-year plan.

If you are able to, go to your nearest store and pick up items to complete a vision board. For a vision board, you will need tape or glue, a cardboard surface, or some type of board to put your vision on, and you will also need magazines. Magazines can be purchased at your nearest thrift store for very little.

If you are able to complete a vision board, we strongly suggest that you give yourself extra time to complete the process, maybe 3 to 5 days. I encourage you to pray before and during the vision board process. The time that we suggest you take to complete your vision board will help you to take your time with the process so that you're not rushing and putting things on there just because. We want you to really take your time, meditate, and understand who you are and what you would like to see based on who you know yourself to be.

The more you know yourself, the better the vision board.
Your vision board will be as detailed as your mind. Throughout the course of this book, we want you to think about executing every calculated step to reach your fiveyear goals and plans.

Section 2: Trusting Completely

In this book, we will focus on making calculated steps. This section focuses on completely trusting God. Now, a lot of people wonder and ask, how do you trust God completely when you're unsure what's going to happen? Well, first and foremost, we have to understand the concept of believing in God (also known as "The Universe") to manifest things into our lives.

To begin to trust completely, the first thing you have to do is have the belief (aka Faith) that you deserve what you desire, that you need what you want, and that you get what you need because the desire is based on purpose. Once you begin to understand what your purpose is and you understand what goals you have set based on: your purpose, character, personality, and who you are, you have to begin to figure out what steps to take to get to the next level and reach your overall goals. When trusting completely, before the first step, you have to understand your process.

So while being set aside, hopefully, you were able to jot down the things that were important to you. If you were able to get your vision board together and/ or write your goal list, then you understand the things that you have for your five-year goals or plans. Next, let's get down to completing a step-by-step process that you believe will get you to your goals.

It's time to complete your vision board. You put on your vision board the things that you would like to complete in the next five years. Your vision board can be set for five years or beyond depending on what you desire for yourself and how you like that plan to be set and go forward.

Now that you've gotten the vision board and or the fiveyear goals, you can set up the step-by-step process. From where you are today, consider the things that you need to learn, and practice, the places that you need to visit to study, and the networks that you desire to have. Begin to take in information that is related to your goals.

If you are figuring out what your purpose is, please go purchase Spiritual Human Behavior. It will help you to evaluate who you are and why, then help you figure out what your individual purpose is. The next thing in
"trusting completely" is "trusting the process."

Understand that your process, path, and goals are not set in stone for you. The process that you set in place (the steps that you believe will take you to where you desire to be) is just a guideline on the things that you know based on your understanding today about what you need to do for the ultimate goal. Understanding that each step will, can, or might shift along the way, depending on what your goals are and what God (The Universe) has set as your purpose, and how those things begin to align.

The more that you align with your goals, purpose, and true divine (most inner self) the easier the process will become. The reason why the process becomes easier is because now you have the alignment that gives you the security of trust to get to where you're going. Know that along this path, there will be challenges, but if you've taken the path that you believe will get you there, then you may want to consider what challenges you may face ahead of time.

When you begin to consider the challenges that you face ahead during the course of the process, you can see where God can make the adjustments while you're on the path to get to your goal. During the course that it takes to get you to your overall goal or to the next level, trust is made up of several components. Trust comes from communication.

Trust comes from prayer. Trust comes from meditation. Trust comes from learning more and doing your part to ensure that any doors that are supposed to open for you can open, as you pursue what's deep down in your core.

Knowing your core is very important. It's knowing the why, to the why, to the why, of why you are who you are and how you got to that point. The more you understand yourself, the more you can understand why your course, path, and journey have been directed to get you to where you're designed to be.

Honestly, everybody does not have the same path because they don't have the same goals. Even when they've been raised in the same household, they can have different journeys to take that will lead them to different places. That does not mean that you won't meet up with anybody that you know, that your journeys might not be similar, or you're not going to be able to supplement the things that you need with the people that are around you.

This is just saying that some people are for a lifetime, meaning they will take the entire course of life with you. Some people are for a season. That means that they're designed to be around but for a little while. And some people are for a reason. They're designed to experience certain things in life with you or be around in a certain period of your life, and then they vacate the premises.

Everybody isn't designed to be with you forever. So you have to be able to get the people that are aligned with your purpose. But the more you understand your purpose; you'll begin to attract the people who fit into your purpose.

When you begin to walk out the course and the plans that God has for your life, the more you will begin to connect and network with people that God may be leading in a similar direction. The overall goal is to focus on being able to trust your journey as you proceed. To calculate those steps, there has to be constant communication with God (The Universe).

Praying on a day-to-day basis to ensure that you're going in the right direction, and making notes of lessons or things that you've learned that will affect the course of your life is very important.

Think about what diminishes your trust, this is the next thing that you have to understand within yourself. Once you figure that out, stay away from the things that diminish the way you trust things like where you're going, why you're going there, and that God told you to be there.

In life, you will experience a lot of people who will question what God told you, not because they're questioning God, but because they're questioning why God hadn't told them. They may be questioning your ability to accomplish something but remember, any reflection that a person makes in most cases is a reflection of who they are and how they think of themselves. So don't hold yourself back based on someone else questioning your ability to do what God told you to do.

With trusting Yourself, you have to build up your confidence so much that nothing that anyone says, that's not directly involved, can diminish what you believe or how you proceed. Because the perception that others have of what God told you should mean nothing to you if those people are not assigned to go on the journey with you. Because a person that is designed to do something totally different may not be able to see what you're designed to do because they were not called to do it.

Nobody has been assigned the privilege or the right to do the things that you were called to do in life. Think about it in every relationship, in every way, what are the things that make you question what you know? What are the things that make you second guess your own self, your confidence, and the things that you discuss with God on a day-to-day basis? Now, if you can tell me the things that diminish your trust, the next step is to tell me why. Okay, so if someone telling you a lie diminishes your trust, the reason why is because it's a lie.

The reason why lies diminish your trust may be because you've experienced so many untruths that led you down a different path and disappointed you that now a lie makes you completely lose trust. There is nothing wrong with that. That is an issue that should be addressed to anybody that lies to you.

So because nobody should have to lie, that already is an issue that's easily addressed. How do you fix having an issue with people lying to you? You simply stop believing their lies. You figure out who the liar is and you stay away from liars.

That's not avoidance. That is making sure you don't put yourself in a situation where you have to question who you are and what you know. If being tardy or late diminishes your trust, understand why the lateness or the tardiness diminishes your trust.

Was there a time that somebody was late and never showed up? Was there a time that somebody was late and it led to disappointment? When you begin to learn why certain things diminish your trust, you can begin to build your trust up in those same areas. You can begin to reinforce trustworthiness within yourself. With trusting completely, you also need to begin to trust yourself.

So that means you need to begin to test yourself. If you believe something, go for what you believe. And if you are not correct, then you're learning how to determine things like what's the difference between when you have anxiety and fear vs when there is a true issue that you're facing that needs to be addressed.

Because fear and anxiety can make things that are not a problem, a problem. This causes fear, anxiety, and the inability to trust. So the goal here is to figure out what emotion is leading your ability to trust. Because if you're walking in love, if you're loving towards others, if you're loving towards yourself, if you built your trust within yourself, then you will be able to determine, is this fear? If this is fear, then I'll move forward.

If this is anxiety based in fear, then I will move forward. If there is an actual problem that needs to be addressed, we will stop, we will address the problem and then we will either reroute or we will move forward. The overall goal is to trust yourself so that you can trust your alignment and you can trust the process of reaching your goals.

When you're able to completely trust, the things that come and might shake or throw off someone unprepared to endure the challenges of a journey won't bother you. You will be able to go and move forward with peace and grace. That peace and grace comes from the ability to trust yourself, to trust the process, having accepted the calculated moves you knew it would take, and also leaving room for grace. Give room for God (The Universe) to say, "These are the steps, going to slide this in here to make it easier," allowing the process to adjust according to your overall goals. Now, in the process of this, your goals may adjust a little bit too, because you may find some other things that you're interested in or want to get into in the course of you making the adjustments to align with your purpose.

Journal Thoughts

Do you trust yourself completely?

Are you capable of pursuing your purpose with your whole heart?

Can you handle the challenges that may come with the process to reaching your goals?

What are three challenges that you may face?

Section 3: Pruning Your Life & Understanding Life Cycles

In this section, you are going to hear about pruning, removing, cutting down, cutting back, optimizing things in your life and understanding the cycles of your life based on the things that you experience. First thing we want to do is help you to recognize, decipher and understand both your weaknesses and what type of distractions are "distractions" for you.

Different people have different weaknesses. What may be a weakness for me may be a strength for you. When I say understanding your weaknesses, it means what makes you feel like you need to grow? What areas do you need to grow in the most? I want you to take your time and write down five things that you consider a weakness.

A weakness does not have to be something that you struggle with completely. It could just be something that you would like to improve in overall. Now that you've written down five different weaknesses, then what are five distractions? A weakness can be different than a distraction because social media can be a distraction, but it can also be something that pushes your brand, your image or helps you grow, communicate, and socialize. It can also be a great learning tool for those that are able and capable of using social media data to learn and reflect on the world around them. So that's not always a distraction for everyone, but what are the things that will throw you off your game? For some people being broke is a distraction. The more you have to focus on ways to get money, the less you can focus on your purpose.

Everybody has a different purpose. Everybody has different distractions. For some people having a child and not having support might be a distraction.

The child itself is not the distraction. The lack of support and being able to adjust your lifestyle so that you can calculate your moves better may be the distraction. In the case where you need to make some adjustments to your lifestyle, then you need to see what the distraction is.

You have lack of support. Maybe you have a lack of childcare options. Then you need to figure out what can you do according to where you're at or according to your weaknesses to begin to strengthen those areas.

Think about being able to create something that you can do that your child can be a part of or if you're in school, discuss with your teachers and instructors about being able to maybe take your child to class with you as long as that child doesn't disturb others. Now, this is just a random weakness, but everybody has different weaknesses. For some, men can be a weakness and a distraction.

For others, women can be a weakness and a distraction. The goal is to figure out what your weaknesses are so that you can gain selfcontrol. Then be able to build yourself up in those areas so that it's no longer a weakness, it is a strength. When you are ready to get into relationships, there will be weaknesses and strengths that both of you possess.

The goal in those type of situations is to get with someone that you don't have to finesse, but someone that sees your best and is able to help supplement the things that you need to work on. Those things will help better the relationship. But when you talk about weaknesses and distractions, you need to figure out what your weaknesses are. You should already know what your strengths are.

If you know what your strengths are and you write your strengths down, then the goal is to become stronger in the weaker areas. When we talk about deciphering your weaknesses, distractions, pruning your life and even life cycles, one of the things that I highly suggest is that you go and look up the characteristics of your Zodiac sign. I know most people don't believe in Zodiacs, but the goal here is to get at least three different Zodiac articles so that you can see the characteristics of people that's born around your birthday and then use those characteristics to help prune your life.

Listen, this is why I say use those things to help prune your life. In the description of your Zodiac sign you will see a list of strengths, a list of weaknesses, you may see some career projections, and some other things. The goal is to use that information to help you understand yourself better as a person born in this particular timeframe and the likeliness of how you can make yourself a better, more mature person. Then understand the things that may be common for somebody that's born around the time that you were born. Check for what you're likely to struggle with. Can you relate to the things that you are struggling with and then learn how to improve those things so that you no longer struggle with the same things over and over again. Honestly, it may sound a bit foolish to go and look at the horoscope if you're not into astrology and horoscopes, but the real truth is that you need to get as many different perceptions of yourself as possible.

You need to figure out all the possible weaknesses and all the challenges that you could face so that you can begin to move a little bit different. You can reinforce positive ways to strengthen yourself, grow and not be the weakest version of yourself with this insight.
The overall goal with faith is to grow into the best version of yourself while reaching goals simultaneously.

Think about this, someone may see social media as something that's draining and a distraction that keeps you away from your goals. The Reality is if you're a person that's pushing a brand or you're advertising and interacting, then social media can be a very good tool to help you establish, build, and effectively get clients for your brand.

Also make sure you are actually into what you are doing, because you realize that you're interested in things that other people may not be interested in. Then you have to be willing to step aside and seek out more information on the things that you actually find interest in. If something inspires you or interest you, it would behoove you to go about seeking more information in that area. Anything that grabs or catches your attention, is something that may be necessary for you to learn in the future, but you might not need it now.

When you get to talking about life cycles, I want you to search the internet and look up "life cycles." There are different numbers associated with your birth date that tell you about who you are and what your "life cycle" will be. There is another website that will give you a list of the actions and things that normally happen around certain times of the year according to your birthday. That is also considered a life cycle. Remember, the goal isn't to focus on numerology, astrology, or any one thing, just like the goal isn't to focus on religion and things that are religious-minded or traditional. The goal is to build yourself up, to know as much as you can so that you can move according to God's plan with the best knowledge possible and to get as much information that will help influence and encourage your faith.

As you begin to understand what's useful, what's purposeful, and what's meant to align you, you will begin to see how some things just simply fade away. Some things won't interest you anymore because it doesn't align with your purpose. So there will be some things that you won't have to "sacrifice."

There will be things that you won't have to and won't seem hard to let go of, because it doesn't align with your purpose. When you begin to align more with your purpose, focusing more on your strengths and strengthening your weaknesses, and you begin to give less attention to things that don't progress you towards your goals, there will be less distractions. There will be less things that drain you because you're using your focus and energy on maintaining the alignment that will get you to your highest version of yourself. When you do this you can reach your goals and you don't have to try to compete or be like anyone else.

So as you move forward, a lot of things will begin to fall away.

Pruning sounds like you're going to take it away, but honestly you have to peel it back.

But as you align with your purpose, the things that try to attach to you will not be able to attach unless they're assigned to you. As you begin to understand the alignment of your assignment, then your mission will become easier. The struggles and the challenges that you face will already be calculated moving forward, allowing you to optimize your confidence by understanding the grace for your purpose. The last thing that I would like to say about life cycles in general is that I want you to take an overview of your life.

I want you to think back over the years, however old you are, and try to group together when you have certain things that happen in your life.

For example over the years, I have learned, paid attention to and noticed that in September, a lot of things happen. I have written down a long list, probably over the last 10 or 15 years of me tracking I have written down at least 50 things that happened in a month of September. I began to realize that there was a cycle because I noticed when things declined, when things increased, when things manifested, and when things began to be planted.

If you're always planting in your life, always feeding yourself, always encouraging yourself, always putting in information, understanding, learning, and growing, then you will always be producing results and manifestations throughout the course of your life. That also means, if you only feed yourself during a certain time, then you'll only receive during a certain time. But if you consistently, monitor the cycles in your life so that you can begin to track when you have highs, when you have lows, and when things are just going with the flow it can be a tool.

Knowing these cycles could help ease your mind a lot because now you know what to look forward to. Every September, I know to look forward to change; whether it's good, bad, or indifferent. I know that change is coming.

Normally the change is good, but not always and it's definitely not easy. Around November, I also see growth and change in establishment. I've also learned that my life cycle starts somewhere in the realms of January, February.

So that means that during those periods, there are certain things that I experience, certain seeds that are being laid so that the ground can begin to harvest whatever I'm manifesting by
September. By November, I begin to see the harvest. If you begin to understand the cycle of your individual life, where things are manifested, in what month do you see most increase, in what month do you see certain things so that you can begin to auto-tune your life to what you know the cycles of your life have determined. And then this, along

with learning your weaknesses, along with seeing what your life path number is, will help you to understand your journey a little bit more.

All of this can help lead to you trusting the path that you're on more as well.

Journal Thoughts

What is it that aligns with your goals in life?

How can you become more efficient in the things that you would like to do?

What is healthy in your life that's helping you reach your goals versus what's draining and keeping you away from reaching your goals?

What helps you align more with your goals?

What classes, what interactions, what mindset will help you to get closer to your goals and in alignment?

Section 4: Conscious Decision-Making

The purpose of this particular section is to help you grow in your decision-making process, to recognize the different patterns of your decision-making and to ensure you are not making irrational unthought-out decisions that could go against your overall plans.

So, what is a conscious decision versus an irrational decision? A conscious decision is a decision that you have thought about, that you are aware of all the consequences, all the possibilities, and all of the actions or reactions that will follow the decision that you are making. Really, this just means that you are weighing out every single option that comes with any decision that you face. The more that you make decisions with a leveled head, weighing out all the possibilities, uncertainties, and all of the consequences, you will begin to make better decisions.

I don't want to say faster, but more accurate and more efficient. As you begin to make decisions based on good things, based on fully thought-out ideals, plans, and according to your purpose and alignment, it actually will help you guide your decisions. If you plan to do things a certain way, steps one through 10, but you get to step three and you have to make a decision that can either propel you further or keep you right on track, what do you choose. Depending on what that decision is, consider that step could have been meant for you to have an enlightening experience of good things.

When you get to step three, if you get a chance to skip to step seven, I want you to really think about what you could be missing. Although that opportunity may seem nice, there may be some things on steps four, five, and six that you may need to experience to take the step seven so that when you get to step eight, you will knock the ball out the park. If you decide to do something irrational because it seems like you may get ahead faster, you might not consider the things that you will experience in steps four, five, and six, or how influential those steps are to the journey. If the decisions and experiences within those steps will help propel you into step seven and eight, then you may miss some good things that can help you advance. Now, an irrational decision is doing something because it seems like it's going to be all right.

Some irrational decisions may work out. A conscious decision may not go as planned, but an irrational decision is something that is extremely spontaneous, that is totally unthought about, and a decision that will affect people in ways that you have not considered. Not just affecting yourself, but affecting those around you.

Lately, we've seen more people experience or hear about mass shootings; most of the time, these young people are making irrational decisions fueled by hate.

That is just an example of an irrational decision because they don't think about the consequences of how it affects others and what the long-term effect will be on themselves. Now, what makes an irrational decision irrational versus a conscious decision? Most times a person acts out of an extreme emotion at a time where you have not taken the time to actually think about the consequences. If you are in a relationship you are likely to experience struggles, I'm not talking about struggle that has to do with abuse, violence or anything in that nature, just typical relationship things that you have to work out.

You have to work through certain parts of your relationship, whether it's the communication, time and attention, or how you are going to move forward together. If you have a tough time communicating, you get pissed off one day, you just storm off, then you don't get the opportunity to actually talk about how you feel. If you don't get to explore why you feel that way, and the things that you would like to do so that you can come together, then you're making an irrational decision to storm off, possibly breaking up over something that's not thought out. This could be something detrimental to your path, purpose, and to the course of life that you see yourself going down. This book started out with you setting your intentions on five-year goals, you need to realize that everything that you do from the time that you set the intention, contributes to your goals. From that moment forward, everything that you decide to do should be a conscious decision that's based in the alignment process of you reaching your goals.

There should not be any task that you are willing to do that is opposite of your goals. What if you have a goal to save $25,000 and you are going towards your goal, then something comes up that is not beneficial, not an investment, and that will in no way possible help you reach new heights. Think about it, doing that vs going forward by saving, only making investable purchases, or investable actions into things that will help you reach your overall goals is an irrational decision.

It is irrational to go and buy a $500 purse when you need to go and invest $500 in your startup for your own business. It is irrational to go and spend $1,200 or $1,600 on a bag when you can be investing that money into a class that can help you to quadruple that. Everything isn't about money and everything is not about business, just like everything isn't about relationships.

Sometimes it's irrational for you to go out to the club when you need to be home studying. You may not be in school, but that doesn't mean that there are not things that you're interested in learning that can further your education, your knowledge or brighten your horizon towards the goals that you have set. The goal is to make conscious decisions, to make decisions that will help propel you into the future that you have planned.

You have to make decisions with intentions in mind. If you have set your intentions or if you have goals that you're trying to reach, then making a decision with your intentions in mind is being mindful of your overall goal. So if you have five-year goals, you still need to be mindful of the things that you have

set out for 10 years, because if your five-year goals get completed in three years, then you still need to be able to say, okay, that went fast. Now, what do we do? How do we continue to strive to be better? How do we continue to meet and grow our expectations within ourselves? How do we not become stagnant and continue to excel to our ultimate goals?
What are your ultimate life goals?

At this step you should have a life plan, not a bucket list of things that you want to do before you die, but have things that you want to reach long-term. One of my long-term goals is to have a book that is published and used for academic purposes. In order to do that, I have to actually either write or record a book such as I am, then publish that book and move forward with the process of getting it accepted in schools.

Now that I've written the book, I don't stop right there at writing the book. Now I have to publish it. Then I have to submit this book to the organizations that will help me get to my overall book goal destination.

Yes, I would like to be a bestseller, but being a bestseller is almost second nature for me to being academically approved for students to learn from the information that I'm putting out there. Of course, you'll be a bestseller if you are an academic, a scholar, someone that is used regularly in the school systems because they have to buy the book by the bulk. Sometimes we may reach our shortterm goals early, but we still have a ways to go to propel to our long-term goals.

So if you make your decisions with the intentions of your goals, hopes, or what you have planned for your family in the future, then you will likely make decisions that are more conscious, more thought out, or planned to help you calculate your steps better. Not making decisions out of desperation is so important because if you make a decision because you desperately need something, you may sign up for more than what you bargained for or more than what you wanted to get yourself into.

So a person that has planned a financial freedom goal to have a little bit of money to further investments, they have to consider where they are and the steps they are willing to take to accomplish their goals.

If a person is completely broke, they may make decisions based on their desperation for money. If a person is lonely and they are desperate for time to spend with someone, they may take time and spend it with the wrong person just to have someone. The goal is to become so full with wholeness and knowledge of who we are and why we are, that whatever decision that we make is a decision of choice.

A decision of choice is the ability to say: I desire that, I want the outcome and I know what I'm getting myself into. Understand that when we make split decisions that are irrational, they're most likely done in desperation. When you do things in desperation, there is a possibility for more people to try to get over on you because they know that you'll do anything for what they have. So a person that will do anything for money, for the right person with the right amount, they're going to sell out.

Realize that it doesn't matter what they're selling out for, if they're doing it solely because they're desperate to get money, there's going to be a lot of things that they'll do just because of money. For people that's desperate to get famous, they will do far beyond what the average person would do to be famous.

Going to get plastic surgery so that you could be accepted by mainstream media is a desperate move to be famous.

I'm not body shaming the girls and guys who have decided to cosmetically enhance their bodies so that they can look and feel better about themselves. But if you're doing it solely for acceptance or surface level reasons, you're not sick, you don't have anything wrong that's causing you to need a procedure, then that seems like a desperate attempt for attention.

If that's your job, I get it. But if you're just doing that to post videos online, to say that you are viral or famous, then that's desperation. A person that is already set will not move at the same level as somebody that is trying to figure out how to get set. When you've established a foundation, you remove the desperation and you can build based on your own terms and condition.

My goal is to help people to live a life on their own terms, not based on what someone else will allow or what someone else says that they should or shouldn't do. My goal is to help make decisions based on how it affects those involved, the person making the decision, their children, and their future. So the biggest thing that I want for you is to see if there's areas where you're desperate for change and then remove that desperation by finding ways to improve that area. So if you're lonely and you find yourself being desperate for attention, then you need to figure out why do you feel lonely? What type of attention are you desperately seeking? And how can you alleviate that need for attention in a way that will not put you in harm's way, around the wrong people or just in a bad place mentally and spiritually. Don't find yourself hanging out with people that are addicts, addictive nature or that will get you into God knows what.

A lot of people that end up on drugs are experimental because they are trying to fill a void or trying to avoid accepting reality.

We don't want you to go to things to escape yourself. You can run from a lot of things but you will never really fully escape yourself. You will only be able to run so long. You will only be able to do but so many drugs. You will only be able to fill your life with void fillers instead of purpose fillers for so long before it begins to wear down on you.
Our goal is to help that not happen.

We don't want life to wear down on you or you to be out here making decisions because you're desperate for change. So, begin to look within, evolve yourself, practice your faith, calculate your steps, then enhance your growth by seeking things that actually influence your affluence and helps you to become a better version of yourself.

What does that mean? Seek out things that you find interest in, whether you want to participate, just want to learn, and grow or you desperately want to be involved. Now, again, the goal for you right now is to remove the nature of desperation. So get yourself familiar with things that interest you.

Once you become familiar with new information, the desperation will leave. The more exposure you have, the less you will feel desperate to jump into something because now you need to know the good and bad, the ups and the downs.

You also need to know the middle ground so that you can know where you fit in the biggest overall picture. Then you need to understand the possibility of the outcomes and the effects of your future. Everything that you do has an effect on somebody.

There is a cause and then there is an effect. There is an action and then there is a reaction. There is a decision and then there is a consequence.

The goal is to help you figure out what consequences come from your decisions before making it. You may make a decision right now, not considering if you want to be married in five years, not considering the possibilities of what could happen in the next five months because you might say you don't want to be married. Then in 10 months, you could meet someone that changes your whole perspective on the situation of marriage.

So before you overcommit to anything, before you sign any long-term contracts for anything, you need to consider within yourself, how will this affect my future? If something comes up between now and the end of this contract, will I be able to take advantage of the things that God may bring into my life? Then make decisions based on how it will affect your future, without limiting your present. You have to understand your why. Everybody has a why.

Every decision comes from a why. Why do you think like that? Why do you decide to do the things that you decide to do? Is there a pattern that you see within decisions that you're making? If you can find the decision-making pattern, then you can change the decisions that you're making and how you make them whenever you don't like the result. The goal is not to just make you change how you make decisions.

The goal is to evaluate the results that you've experienced in your life, whether material, physical, financial, spiritual, or mental, then look at the results that you have. Look at where your life is right now today and begin to see where you can calculate things differently so that you can get a different result? Because the definition of insanity is doing the same exact thing over and over and over again and expecting a different result, but you've changed nothing. So if you begin to understand your why, why do you want to set this goal? What does it mean to you and your family? What does this 5-year plan mean to you and your family? And then if you understand your why beyond legacy, beyond financial growth, what do you see your purpose being? Why do you believe that that's your purpose? Why do you want to submit to the call of your purpose? What are you expecting from what you're doing? Is there an outside expectation or is there an inner growth expectation? Then plan out the possible outcomes for every decision that you make.

Honestly, every decision that the owners of Speaking Freedom have made, there has been a plan or an acknowledgement of the things that could go right and the things that could go wrong. Whether you're building a family, starting a business, writing a book, becoming a mom, moving to a new city, what are the things that can go right? What are the things that could go wrong? How can you pre-plan for correcting mistakes, errors, failures, and things that are out of your control? Determine your decision-making thought patterns. How do you think about the things that you have to make a decision about? Are you thinking about the negative (fear-based, false evidence appearing real)? Or are you thinking about the facts that you can achieve anything that you can put your mind to, if you can figure out how to solve whatever problem that it presents? When you begin to find your consistencies, what are your consistent patterns of decision-making? And how have those patterns of decision-making affected your life? Is there any area that you say, you know what? I might've been a little bit irrational right there.

Then figure out what made you become irrational in that decision-making process. If you're a person that falls in love easy, what is making you fall in love so easy? What is it about a man that makes you fall head over heels? If you continue to fall head over heels for the wrong type of gentleman, why? What can you do differently to help protect yourself and safeguard yourself from falling head over heels too fast? If you are a man who does not know how to say no to a woman, what is it that that woman does that is making you feel like you cannot say no? For some men, if you stop having sex with a woman, they may feel like they have no more power over you. I'm not telling you to stop having sex with women for the rest of your lives, but I'm saying if you withhold yourself, your money, and the things that people are depending on you for, how will those same people treat you? How would you guys move different together? Women, if you did not allow for men to feel like they could be so up close and personal, how would that affect your decision-making process? The point is you have to find your weakness.

You have to identify the areas of distraction for you in your decision-making process. Because if you see one shiny thing and that makes you change your mind, then you need to dull your arousal for that shiny thing. You may not need to totally dislike it, but you need to not allow that to be a distraction to your growth, your increase, your wisdom, your knowledge, or your spiritual evolution.

What are your consistencies in decision-making? How do you make decisions? What is your first thought before you decide on something? Do you consider how it will affect your children if you have children? If you're single, your decision-making needs to be focused on what do you want out of life long-term? Your decisions as a single person, especially if you're single, not married, no kids, then your decisions are based on how they will affect you long-term. Do you want children? How is the things that you're doing now building your life to be able to sustain the lifestyle that you want long-term? Those things will help you make better decisions. How does the decision affect the effects of those around you? Sometimes we make a decision and we don't even think about how it will affect the people around us.

Not what effects them only physically, but how will it make them think? How would it change their overall perception of the world? If you're a parent and you do something irrational, if you go to jail, how does that affect your child long-term? If you already have a criminal history, there's some things that you cannot do anything to change. However, how you move going forward says a lot. I'll use an example of Meek Mill.

Meek Mill had a criminal record. Now his criminal past has been dismissed. However, it took him taking the steps to be a better person in order for that to come underway.

He had to go through the process of going to jail, being falsely accused, and enduring the long period of probation sentencing. But going through all of that helped make him to be a better version of himself. I believe that most of his struggle was because he had made some decisions that was triggering an effect of other things that had taken place prior.

So when you begin to make decisions that can affect your now because of your past, you have to really decide, okay, how is popping a wheelie going to affect me? Because for Meek Mill, it sent him back to prison. Overall, that probably was the one thing that helped bring attention to his case. Who goes to jail for popping a willy? But that one decision, or just one decision going out of town when you're on probation without permission can send you back to jail.

Before you go and do a crime, think about the time that you will have to spend correcting that wrong, the time that you will have to spend possibly in jail. Think about the karma that comes with it. And not just criminals, this is just any type of thing that you're doing.

How does it affect you long-term? How does it affect your future decisions, your environment or your legacy and your long-term commitments? There are a lot of people that get in the spotlight, but as soon as you get in the spotlight, people will go and find everything that you've ever said bad and use that against you. We don't want you to stop being you in fear that somebody will use it against you, but we want to make sure that you are the best you so that there is nothing that people can use against you.

When you begin to see your decisions as conscious or irrational, we hope that you make more conscious decisions, considering how it will affect your goals, how it reflect in your lifestyle, how it will affect your family and your children, your soul, and your purpose. There are some decisions that you will make that will make you feel inadequate because you know it's not in alignment with your purpose. There are some decisions that you can make that will have an after effect that you don't notice until you see it down the line later. So before you make any decisions, especially if you're in music or in any type of entertainment, think about the decisions that you're making. Think about the contracts that you're signing before you sign them so that you can ensure that you are maintaining your right to freedom, your right to creativity and your right to your own art.

Journal Thoughts

How can you make better conscious decisions?

How can you make a decision that will change your life long-term while considering things that you're doing now?

Every little thing that you do now counts towards your long-term. Even though it seems like a whole bunch of small things, every decision counts towards where you're going.

Feel Free to answer questions from throughout this chapter as well.

Section 5: Understanding God's Love When Calculating Faith Moves

Now, as you begin to exercise your faith, make calculated moves, begin to trust God completely, and prune your life of the unnecessary negative things, you're going to have to begin to actualize God's love for you while walking out your faith. This is going to be very important because as you begin to walk out your faith in your calculated moves, you are going to begin to face challenges and the challenges will vary.

For some, the challenges will be overcoming self. For others, challenges will be overcoming the feeling of being alone as you're growing, set aside, and moving towards your purposeful alignment. When you begin to understand God's love for you through the course of your path to purposeful alignment, you will begin to see yourself as God sees you.

Understand why you've been chosen. Understand that you were the person that God knew would carry out the purpose that is within you. A lot of that has to do with shaking off and removing a lot of the judgment, conditioning, and turning yourself down or off to make others comfortable around you.

When you began to see yourself as God sees you, you began to understand your own unique light. You began to appreciate the gifts that you recognize within you while moving forward.

This particular section is positioned here because the next step is to begin to understand your gifts, your light and learning how to execute those things despite what people say, despite what people feel and despite what you see sometimes.

You need to be able to gain the confidence and the love that God has placed within you and for you, so that when you begin to walk out these calculated moves, exercise your natural gifts and walk into your purpose, nothing can faze you. The goal is for nothing to be able to deter you, to tear you down or make you second guess yourself outside of needing to readjust the plan.

Now, see yourself without flaws. See yourself as a person with a soul that has manifested into the body that you're in. See everything that you've ever endured as a part of the course to get you to your destiny. When you think about things like that, you may wonder, well, why did this or that happen? What I want you to consider is if that thing happened to you or if the way you handled it made it seem like it was a negative experience, look at it differently. Depending on your age and what your life experiences are or have been, the effect of each thing that you've endured will begin to resonate with you differently as you begin to accept it as a part of your path that got you to where you are today.

If you can learn and grow from the things that felt like a burden or moments of failure, then you will begin to embrace those as moments of lessons that were miscalculated before. If you begin to see yourself without flaw, if you begin to embrace yourself as though God placed you in every situation to grow you, how could that thinking change your life for the better? How could you see your five-year goals manifest? Because God's love is birthed in self-love, if you do not love yourself, you cannot properly love God and you won't see the love that God has within you, because you don't see love within yourself.

You cannot believe that God values you more than you see value in yourself, so find the value in yourself. I am not talking about the value based on the amount of cash you have in your bank account.

I am not talking about the value based on the shoes, the clothes, the car you drive, or the food that you eat. I'm not even talking about the value that comes from the job that you work to get the money that you have. What is the value of your soul? What do you naturally bring to this earth? Where does your good vibes resonate from and how do they resonate you into your truth? You have to see yourself as God sees you.

How does God see you? As a soul who is experiencing life for the first time in this body, unless you are the type of person who seeks to do past life regressions. If you're not the person that seeks to go to spiritual advisement to get further help to understand how you got in this position in this lifetime, than you need to accept that this is your first time on this planet, in this body, as this soul. The things that you've been sent to this planet for will resonate within your soul and everything that you experience is to help you grow and to help you grow the people around you. For myself, I always reflect and say, if everything that I've gone through was to teach somebody else how to get through, then I've served my purpose on earth because I've been through a lot.

When you've gone through a lot, you can begin to help other people get through a lot too. Even if they're not going through the same exact thing, learning how to overcome adversities is across the board and can be applied to any given area of your life. You can grow from any topic, any level of decision-making, or anything that will affect your life greatly.

One of the hardest things to accept is that everything that we've gone through was designed to help us develop sustainability and the capability to get through life and live our purpose based on what the circumstances have created us to be. So you have to understand that you were made with a purpose, even if you can't see how the challenges have helped you grow just yet. I say just yet, because if you begin to look and reflect on how you have been influenced and changed by the circumstances of your upbringing, you will begin to see where things made you stronger, more observant, more alert, and more aware of who you are when you did not have to turn yourself off.

Even if you think of the things that you were conditioned to think nothing of or turn yourself off to, you will begin to see different parts of you. You will begin to embrace the many forms of who you are within your soul realizing that it's multidimensional, multifaceted and all encompassing. We tend to turn parts of ourselves off to fit the environment around us instead of allowing ourselves to flourish so the environment can adjust to us.

Once we do that we can be in the places that we should be and not force ourselves to be in places that don't allow us to feel God's love within, that makes us reject or question ourselves. The goal is to build your confidence in the love of God within you so that you can know that nothing outside of you can tear you down. The love of God through self-love will align the mind to walk out the steps in your life.

The more you love yourself, the more you will become okay with making decisions that might piss other people off but will take you closer to your purpose. You will make decisions with confidence that may make others uncomfortable but will walk you right down your path to soul salvation, self-love, and worthiness for you. The thing that we collectively have to understand is that we were made individuals.

God never intended for everybody to be exactly the same. In order for you to embrace who you are as an individual, you have to love yourself. You have to appreciate everything that you've endured that made you who you are, then build confidence in who you are because of everything that you overcame.

How has that developed your character? Well, you're going to need a lot of self-love in order to get through the necessary steps of faith to see your five-year goals. For the intentions that you set throughout your life, you're going to need faith. It takes faith and confidence from self-love to do something different to see different results unless you want the exact same things as everybody else. The truth of the matter is what makes someone else happy, might not make you happy.

Somebody else's five-year goals might be burdensome on you because you don't know their path, their calling, their gifts, their talents, and you don't know what part of themselves that they are diminishing or rejecting just to appease what the world says should be popular. The goal is self-acceptance, self-love and confidence so that you can move forward strong, so that you can have peace of mind about everything with every decision that you have to make coming up. Loving on yourself on a new level provides a new level of confidence.

That doesn't mean that you don't love anybody else, that you don't let anybody in, that nobody else is capable of loving you or showing you how to love yourself better. The truth of the matter is that when you begin to love yourself, the love that you have for yourself reflects in all the relationships around you. Those relationships will turn into love sprouting relationships, blossoming other loving relationships, that will blossom other loving relationships. Now, I know it seems like I repeated myself three times but I'm talking about three different cycles of loving relationships that are created.

As you begin to initiate self-love, you ignite the empowerment for someone else to love themselves authentically. When you begin to embrace your gifts, your calling, to make better decisions, to go against the norm, against the standards of society, or to walk in the fullness of who you are, you give permission to your daughter, your mother, your sister, and your cousins. When you Love yourself, you give permission to every single person on this earth that you encounter to walk more proudly in who they are, to accept themselves, to love themselves and extend the love branch to others. When they see you able to love yourself and they love themselves, someone sees them loving their selves, then they begin to love themselves and the trickling of love expands and spreads. So although we're talking about loving ourselves more, when we love ourselves more and better, we love others better.

And as we love others better, they begin to love themselves more, love themselves better and love others better. That's how you spread self-love, self-reliance, and self-confidence on earth.

Journal Thoughts

How could you love yourself better?

What are some things that God placed within you?

What are some things that God allowed your mind to think or allowed you to experience throughout the course of your life that you could Look at different, that can help you understand yourself better so you can love yourself better because if you understand yourself, you can love yourself.

Write down five areas where you could love yourself better, where you could accept yourself more, where you can embrace yourself, be yourself and free others to be their selves as well.

Section 6: Walking in Your Faith

I don't want this to seem redundant.

However, I do want you to understand what it means to walk out your faith. So walking out your faith is actually exercising the various things that you've learned in the last several sections and in previous books. When you begin to walk out your faith, you're saying, okay, now it's time to apply the things that I've learned thus far in life.

Gaining faith and gaining faith in God within you is about learning your universal uniqueness while learning to trust the natural essence of who you are.

Everyone is different. Everyone is designed to be different. So for you to walk out your faith, you have to recognize who you are, and recognize what you believe you are purposed on this earth for.

The vision boards should help you recognize your purpose. The more time that you spend meditating, the more time you spend developing, the more you'll align to what your faith is supposed to be and how to walk that out. So now that you've gotten the steps, now that you have gotten a better understanding of conscious decisionmaking, now that you're understanding the love that God has placed within you, how do you decide to walk out your faith? It depends on what you are believing for in faith.

When setting your intentions on your five-year goals, you begin to take the steps within the plan that you're aligning with. As you continue to align with that plan, your faith is developed with each step and more of the plan is revealed. As you step, something else happens.

It's like a maze where every time you make a step forward, the maze shifts. Every time you step on a new block, the maze shifts. Every time you walk out a little further in faith, every time you test your endurance a little bit more, the course of your life shifts.

As the course of your life shifts and the path is made aligned, every decision shifts in alignment as you begin making conscious decisions. When you begin to love the conscious decisions that you make because you've learned to love the God within you, you know that God will never fail you. You also know that the universe will never send you down a path of doom and destruction as long as you continue to align with your purpose. So what is your purpose? What are the things that you feel drawn to? What inspires you? What makes your soul feel rejuvenated? What makes your mind want to grow more and go further? Because the God in you will be ignited by the things that are purposeful to your path, to your individual journey and your individual course in life.

Now, if you're a person that has ever read the Bible or knows the reference in the Bible that says, "before God (The Universe) created you in your mother's womb, God (The Universe) knew you." I read something once that said every egg that your mother was ever going to carry or birth was in her when she was formed in her mother's belly. That means that she was in the egg of her grandmother's belly and every egg that has ever been birthed went through generations before it was birthed, experiencing things while in the womb. This could be the link to the life cycles, your soul cycles or being born to certain levels of soul depth. Because if you experienced a life through the womb of a womb of a womb of a womb, then that's knowledge on top of knowledge on top of knowledge on top of knowledge being passed down within your DNA upon your birth, and presence on this earth.

Those are the things that help shape you, your purpose, your path, and your walk. As you begin to gain faith in yourself, understand the love that's in you, accept God's call and God's path that you begin to walk out step by step, you will begin to notice the doors opening, the connections being made, the little things that you paid no attention to before, now have meaning and makes sense.
This helps you to continue to move forward in your faith, operating in more faith as you see your faith working.

See faith is not faith until you have an action behind it.
You can believe all you want to. Belief alone is not faith.

Faith is what you practice. Faith is what's applied to your life and exercised so that it strengthens you, grows you and modes you into the person that you are meant to be on this path. Become confident in what to believe in and what you believe in.

I suggest strongly, no matter your race, your religious preference, or what you've been exposed to, you should begin to do research on what you believe so that you can know why you believe what you believe. You should have some reference points aside from one unobjectable book. You need to have history and understand how history has prepared you for now if you're open to grow from history.

It's best if you allow your results to be somewhat of a guidance to where your faith moves you. If you're believing for something and you begin to take the steps for that, you will start to see the manifestation happening as you take steps, but be sure to have alignment checkpoints. As everything around you progresses, you start seeing the signs everywhere that things are going in your favor and doors open, then naturally you go where favor takes you. When you are moving forward you will see your favor shift based on the steps that you need to take and you might have to shift what you're doing. Remember this journey is about always developing, growing, learning and applying what you know. Having a lot of knowledge but not applying it is useless information and a waste of time.

When you use every aspect of every experience for growth you can walk with the most utmost confidence and obtain the promises of God as you feel drawn to things with your mind (spirit), your heart (soul) and body (vessel). The soul guides the body to where it belongs when in alignment. An essential part and the key to actually walking out your faith is understanding your distractions. While you're walking out your faith there will still be things that will come up to try to convince you to leave the course that you're taking, to go a different way, to take a shortcut, to do all these things to distract you. Focus on the favor, focus on the signs, the wonders, the things that you begin to see manifesting and follow the path.

It's like following the yellow brick road. As you begin, the road is laid out for you but if you don't walk, the road will not appear before you even though the road is already there waiting on you. That's what faith is.

Faith is walking the road and the road being laid out with every step. As you begin to realize that the steps that you take determine the road that you go down and the path that you end up on, you'll begin to use all of the skills, techniques, and knowledge that you're obtaining now to help guide you and perfect your individual faith walk. A lot of people will tell you that you have to do this or that but your walk with God in this universe, on this journey of life may not be equivalent to anybody else's walk.

You have to take your steps to understand where you were supposed to be. For me, I joined the military and several other people I know joined the military, but none of the people that I know had the same course, went to the same places that I went or experienced the same things that I experienced. My path in the military was specifically for me.

There was nobody else that could take my assignments because they were my assignments. And that's the way that you have to look at your Life. If faith was your "military," would you be able to handle the assignment that's been given to you. Could you walk the path out despite what it looks like, how it appears to be, and the judgment of others? Can you continue walking down that path? Can you continue to tune out the distractions? Have you noticed as you grow that distractions change with your interests, but how something else presents as a distraction?

Can you tune out the new things that try to get your attention to distract you from your strides in faith? You can start off taking baby steps, but we're not taking baby steps the entire way. Eventually you get into a stride with long, big steps because you're sure of yourself. The more sure of yourself you become, the more you can run your race in faith.

Journal Thoughts

How can you exercise and walk in your faith better?

Name five things that you can do to walk out your faith and to walk in love.

What are the things that you believe that you need to become more confident in so that nobody can shake your faith?

List two steps that will open up a door or could open up a door for you by living your faith, by breathing your faith, by walking out your faith.

What is your next faith walk step?

Section 7: Exploring Your Gifts and Your Talents

This section may be a little overwhelming for some depending on who you are, especially if you have suppressed your natural capabilities in your physical body on this earth. Everybody is born with natural capabilities: some people run fast, type fast, are naturally acrobatic, great at writing, acting, articulating the knowledge that they acquire, computer programming and some are good builders.

On the spiritual side, there are people who are prophetic, foresee the future, are mediums who can sense spirits around them, some dream things that happen, feel other people's energy, and feel sickness to name a few.

There are all types of different talents, gifts, and skills. To begin to explore your gifts, you have to see what you do naturally and what flows naturally. If people come to you for advice all the time, you may naturally give good advice.

If people come to you or if you always know the best dance moves, you may naturally be a great

dancer. If you have the ability to speak in tongues or pray without ceasing, then you may be a prayer warrior for someone.
Now, your gifts and your talents can be both spiritual and physical.

There are some things that you are physically capable of doing that nobody else is physically capable of doing, but there are spiritual things that your soul is purposed to do on this earth, and those are the things that we want to tap into the most. What do you do naturally? What is your natural disposition? What is your natural way of thinking? What is your natural talent? If you don't know, begin to explore your interests.

What do you like to do? Do you like to draw? Do you like to sing? Do you like to do things that helps you feel more connected to the earth and makes your soul feel alive? Identify what your gift is.

There is a section in spiritual human behavior that speaks on gifts, talents, and skills very deeply. But in this particular book, we are learning how to recognize our gifts and talents, then how to use them in faith.

Your purpose will connect directly to your gifts and your talents and your gift is supposed to make room for you. Whatever you do naturally is what you should be doing every day, and it should be done regularly. I'm not telling you to quit your job to follow your passion or your gift. However, if you are able to secure your financial future, so that you can begin to practice your gift more often or can make time to practice, do so.

But do not use this book as an excuse to why you quit your job to explore your gifts if you're not capable of sustaining yourself after you quit. But your purpose connects you directly to your gift. Your purpose may come through trial and error of using your gift.

If a person likes to write for a hobby but doesn't want to write full time, they might not realize that writing is the gift that makes room for you to do other things. Your purpose may not necessarily be writing, but something that may take written effort to start. Put your gift and skills to work, even if you are nervous. As a person who dreams and those dreams oftentimes manifest into reality, one of the hardest things that you could do is begin to exercise your gift, especially if it's a prophetic or spiritual gift that may make others uncomfortable. Some gifts may make others look at you differently because they've been convinced that it's spooky, evil or something of the sort.

But this is where I need you to apply the confidence in who God created you to be and go do research about your spiritual gifts. Do research on your talent and craft. You have to make the mental investment into your spirit so that your spirit can feed your soul so that your soul can pump that back into your spirit mind.

As you begin to feed your purpose within your soul, it will rejuvenate the whole essence of your being. Your whole life will begin to feel new because you're tapping in the purpose of you. Even if you're nervous, take a chance on your natural abilities and spiritual gifts. In order for you to become more confident in your gifts, you will have to practice your gifts. In order for you to practice your gifts, you may have to do it either physically or virtually.

For some, you need physical contact with people or with whatever it is your gifting is leading you and guiding you to. Allow peace to be your umpire even in nervousness, even in anxiety as you practice your gift. If you are a singer, that's a gift, practice your gift. You don't necessarily need vocal training, but you do need to sing in order to train your vocals. If you are a person that's great administratively, that may be a spiritual gift because there is a huge calling that God needs for everybody to do what they're good at in the earth.

There is something that you are good at that if you do it, you will change lives. It may be other people that do what you do, but they are not you. There are certain people that you are called to have influence in their lives.

Someone else is called to make a difference in somebody else's life. One person can't reach the entire universe, but the universe can be fed through one person. Somebody has to be willing to walk out their gifts and practice because practice makes greatness.

You have to be willing to trust in who God called you to be because if you have the gift, then God gave it to you. The God that I know would not give you a gift that you were not designed to use and that he didn't need for you to use right now in this time, which is why you're here today. You're listening to this as confirmation to walk in your light and to shine bright, not like a diamond because a diamond reflects, but if you're reflecting the image of God, then shine like a diamond.

You have a natural gift and talent; you have to be confident in it. For some instances, it will take you into doors and places that you never imagined. You might need to go in a strip club and help somebody come out of the strip club.

You may need to go in a prostitution ring and help somebody come out of prostitution. You may need to go to the homeless people and help people understand their souls and gifts, so they no longer have to be homeless. Your gift may be in politics so that you can change policies that change the world that we live in.

Everything that we have established in this world was created by a person who had an ideal, a gift, a talent, and they did it. They walked out the faith of the love in God, so that they can be great. You have to know that your gift is for both you and the community.

Don't be selfish with your gift. God gave you that because God figured that you would use that for good. Don't use your greatness to cause havoc in someone else's life.

Use your gift to promote growth. Use your gift to help the community become better. Your purpose is tied into your gift.

If you hold back on your gift, you're holding back on yourself. You're denying yourself. For if you deny one portion of yourself, you've denied your whole entire self because you are one whole person and every single portion of you needs to be accepted, embraced, and lived out, even if it's something that you don't understand.

Do your research. Figure out what are you naturally drawn to?

What do you naturally do great? And explore that thing until you realize how that was placed in you for something more purposeful than you may be able to see currently.

Honestly, a lot of people struggle with their gifts and their talents, especially if they're of a spiritual nature because when we're smaller, normally we're told that we're not experiencing what we are experiencing.

We are told to bottle that energy up and to denounce it in most cases. But if you're an adult or a teenager and you are able to begin to exercise your gift, please do so. Now, I want to foolish prove this because sexual nature is a gift, but we do not want you to use sex as your gift to advance in life.

We do not want you to sell any of your gifts and talents for money in a way that you are not able to be free, allowing God to use you and your gift in this earth.

Journal Thoughts

What do you do naturally?

How can you use what you do naturally to help the community as well as yourself?

How can you grow your natural abilities?

What information can you search out and find?

Who can you connect to that can help you develop your particular gift? I don't know your gift. Only you know what you're good at.

Only you know what you do naturally, second nature without a second thought and it's always on point. Only you can tell you that. Unless someone is around you to see you on a regular basis, another person can't tell you your gift unless they're spiritually gifted to help you identify that.

Understand who you are. You may be a healer. You may be a prophet.

You may be something else that is yet to be explored. Your gift may be in fashion. Your gift may be in confidence.

Your gift may be in purpose. Find your gift, love your gift, and use your gift.

Section 8: Faith and Integrity

I know that I told you that you should be working on your vision board but I should have probably said to actually complete the board after you finish this book. Before you create your vision or your vision board, commit to doing whatever it takes to completing whatever comes from your vision board. This can sound a little bit daunting or scary because you don't know what you're creating yet.

You don't know what God has placed in you just yet but whatever is in you, you're capable of completing. Whatever vision that God has given you, he's already equipped you for fulfilling that vision.

Say this aloud:

"I commit to carrying out the purpose, plan and vision for my life and nothing that I will do will stop me from carrying out the purpose, plan, and vision for my life.

My vision is a priority. My vision includes God, my family, my purpose, and my lifestyle. My purpose is my gift, my family, my faith and ensuring that I do my part to impact the world in a positive way."

As you begin to create the vision board, as you begin to hone in, think about and meditate on what's important to you, what your gift, talent and skill are, what do you do naturally. When you begin to assess who you are, where you desire to be and what God created you to experience (the testimonies you can help others with) you will become more clear about your vision.

The vision board is just to help you to get out what's inside of you. It's the things that float around your head about your potential. It's a way you can see your potential in front of you on a board or on paper, so that you can begin to live up to living out the purpose within you. As previously stated, you have to commit that no matter what, you will always be committed to the purpose that God has placed within your soul over your life and allow your spirit mind to connect and be guided by that purposeful light. Be willing to set boundaries, know what you're willing to do and know what you're not willing to do.

That's the "integrity factor." There are things that can be available because of who you are, your purpose, your gifts, skills, and talents. People see when you enter a room the light that you shine and how things are drawn to you. It's like a moth to a flame and you have to be willing to set your boundaries. Just because something is made available to you does not mean that you should be indulging in it or that it's for you. As you begin to be successful, you have more options, but having more options does not mean selecting those new options. It means although more things are available, everything that is available won't be what's best for you. Some things are designed to test your integrity.

When I think of the integrity factor, I think of people who have done questionable things and they think at the moment that they've gotten away with it, especially when it comes to your purpose, your life, and your career. As you begin to move forward, sometimes those things can come back to haunt you. This is where the integrity of your faith comes in because if you've walked with integrity, then there will be very little that people will be able to use against you in regard to your faith. I know you're not perfect, nobody on this earth is.

Not even Jesus was perfect based on man and human standards, he was condemned and persecuted for his actions. Your purpose allows for you to have grace in God's eye. There are some things that you were graced for because your purpose is towards that area.

Your alignment sends you down a path that others may not be able to make it through, that others may not be called to be on, but you have to set your perimeters. Your boundaries about how you're going to walk out your purpose, how you're going to live once success knocks on your door. Once the door is open, what do you know that you're absolutely not going to do just because you're successful and is made available to you? Set your boundaries. Set the boundaries of things that you allow to come in and what you will put out.

It's not always about what people are offering you, but also what you're offering people. Don't start out saying, I am not going to do this because my integrity or other people questioning my integrity, then turn around and do the very thing that you said that you wouldn't do because integrity.

As I have entered my role as a life enhancement coaching specialist to both celebrities and noncelebrities, what I have noticed the most is that to become famous, you have to be you. You have to be confident.

You have to be sure. However, there are a lot of people, especially in the social media age, that believe that to be famous, you have to look a certain way, they will go and get whatever body work that they believe will make them be more acceptable, more presentable, sometimes for their own desire to have more confidence in themselves.

Those same people go out and sell workout videos. That's not integrity because you are never going to get another person to look like something with exercise that you wouldn't paid for. So if ever somebody comes and says, "Well, you didn't work out, your integrity is on the line because you're selling something that you didn't earn the way that you're trying to sell it.

Integrity works in various ways, but it's being who you are and about your word regardless. It's about having boundaries and making sure that you stick to your plan, that you stick to the basis in which you and God agreed upon how you will move forward. Commit to doing whatever it takes to fulfill the purpose on your life.

Honestly, the purpose on your life should not take you into anything that will harm you. I cannot say that it won't place you in questionable situations to other people, but to God and the universe, your path is aligned with the grace for your life. What God may want you to do may look questionable to other people, but we're here to please God, and to be in total alignment with God in this universe.

If people don't understand your walk, that's their problem. Your faith walk is between you and God. I want you to be encouraged to have integrity about everything that you do, about everything that you say, and about how you move forward in your purposeful way.

What I don't want you to do is condemn people for things and then go back and do the same thing that you condemned other people for. People will say you're a hypocrite, but it's a matter of integrity. So for myself, I try not to judge people, one, because I don't want that judgment on myself, but also because I don't know what the future holds.

I won't limit God, maybe according to my future, based on what I know my purpose is and how I'm aligning with it. Because as you align, you will see a broader perspective of what God has for you. What the universe has sent you to this earth for may be a little bit bigger than what the people that are around you can comprehend.

You have to know your capacity. What can you handle? What will be too much for you? Your faith will not push you beyond what you can handle.

Your faith is not going to tell you to go try crack and then you'd be strung out on crack while you're talking about, I'm exercising my faith. That is not exercising your faith. It's no integrity and you saying, well, in order to get them off of drugs, I'm going to try drugs.

You don't try drugs to get people off of drugs. You provide a better way so that they don't have to go down that path anymore. It's like, if I tell you that your dress is too tight, then I should be able to provide something that may be just as sexy, but a little less fitting.

As far as tightness, the integrity factor keeps you on up and up with God more than it keeps you on up and up with people. Your word with God is stronger than anything else on this earth. Because you may commit to something with someone and then the Holy Spirit (God's whole spirit, the universal energy that has created us and cultivated us into love, by love, for love) may lead you to do something different than what you already agreed to.

That's why we take decisions to God first. We meditate on things before we make a big jump, a big leap, a decision that will affect us long-term. Set your boundaries, commit to whatever it is that it will take to fulfill the purpose and vision upon your life.

You may make decisions in the course of what you're doing, pursuing your purpose that may make variances of what may need to be adjusted in order for the fulfillment of the things that you've said that you desire in your life. In Faith 301, the next book, you will be given more information about how this applies to love, in love and faith. So, but right now we want you to know your capacity.

What's too much for you? You got to know what's too much for you so you don't get in over your head. You got to know if you have an addictive nature. You have to know if you have an OCD type nature.

You have to know what you can get in, what you can handle and what may be too much. Now, this isn't about fear or you not living up to your potential or you limiting God. It's about knowing the strength of your mind and knowing what you can handle if you get into something or how to get out of something.

Consider what it will take to advance. Do your research. Understand what the vision that you're creating is asking of you.

You're asking your soul for the vision and in order to carry out that vision, your soul is asking something of you. Be willing to walk in that vision with integrity. Keep your word to yourself and God before you keep your word to anybody else, by doing what you say you'll do. If you keep your word to God and yourself, you will become trustworthy to you, and you'll never second guess yourself because of anything presented.

You need Faith and integrity.

To be able to walk out your faith in its highest potential, you have to have integrity with God and with yourself more than anybody else. The integrity factor is based on what you do or do not do and how it can come back later to haunt you. So you need to be solid.

I believe in karma, what you put out there is what you get back. It's like the law of attraction but it's more of a physical nature, with energy.

If you are a good person, then be a good person, have integrity about deciding to be a good person, live that good person image, not as an image but as your purpose.

Create your lifestyle based on your faith, your integrity, your ability to create a vision, see a vision, catch God's vision for your life and then carry that vision out.

Journal Thoughts

How could you have more integrity in regards to your faith?

How can your integrity help you identify your purpose?

What can you do in the utmost solid way, that will not make you question yourself or God?

What have you learned about vision, about meditation, about decision-making, about walking in your faith and exercising and exploring your gifts that will take your life to the next level?

Vision Board Assignment

If you already went and obtained all of the material to complete your vision board, I would like for you to take time to meditate.

If you are a person that believes in the Bible, get your favorite scripture, the scripture that you would like for your lifestyle to be based on and allow that to be the foundation of your vision board. From there, begin to look through your magazines and see what resonates with your soul. Everybody's vision board will be different.

For some people, it will be a lot of words. For other people, it will be pictures. For some people, your vision board may be small or it may start out very thin.

When I say thin, because it's somewhat of a collage type of effort, it may not have everything at once. If you take the three to five days to complete it, you should be able to create and meditate and explore the depths of your heart within those three to five days. You should see a very well-conceived vision board for yourself.

And then pray about it. For at least the first three to four months, look at your vision board every day. Embrace what your vision board shows you and what it says.

And then be willing to open your mind to what it will take in order to fulfill the vision for your life. Your five-year plan is capable. Your five-year plan can be completed before five years.

Your ability to walk in your purpose is all in you. You just have to be willing to walk it out by faith.

Thank you for your purchase. Please purchase our other books:

Spiritual Human Behavior
Faith 101
Faith 301
Faith 401
The Unknown Power of a New Believer
It's My Time

www.ingramcontent.com/pod-product-compliance
Lightning Source LLC
Chambersburg PA
CBHW070155080526
44586CB00015B/2006